Classic Dylan.

A collection of all the music from four landmark Dylan albums.
Arranged for piano/vocal with guitar frames and full lyrics.

Amsco Publications
New York/London/Sydney

Order Number AM 80185
US International Standard Book Number: 0.8256.1289.6
UK International Standard Book Number: 0.7119.2330.2

Exclusive Distributors:
Music Sales Corporation
257 Park Avenue South, New York, NY 10010 USA
Music Sales Limited
8/9 Frith Street, London W1V 5TZ England
Music Sales Pty. Limited
120 Rothschild Street, Rosebery, Sydney, NSW 2018, Australia

Printed in the United States of America by
Vicks Lithograph and Printing Corporation

Blonde On Blonde.

Rainy Day Women #12 & 35

Words and Music by Bob Dylan

stone ya when you're try'n' to go home._____ Then they'll

stone ya when you're there all a - lone._____ But I

would not___ feel___ so all a - lone,_____

Ev - 'ry-bod - y must get stoned._____ 2. Well, they'll

5. F D°7 C7/E

Ev - 'ry - bod - y must get

F

stoned.

Additional Lyrics

2. Well, they'll stone ya when you're walkin' 'long the street.
They'll stone ya when you're tryin' to keep your seat.
They'll stone ya when you're walkin' on the floor.
They'll stone ya when you're walkin' to the door.
But I would not feel so all alone,
Everybody must get stoned.

3. They'll stone ya when you're at the breakfast table.
They'll stone ya when you are young and able.
They'll stone ya when you're tryin' to make a buck.
They'll stone ya and then they'll say, "Good luck."
Tell ya what, I would not feel so all alone,
Everybody must get stoned.

4. Well, they'll stone you and say that it's the end.
Then they'll stone you and then they'll come back again.
They'll stone you when you're riding in your car.
They'll stone you when you're playing your guitar.
Yes, but I would not feel so all alone,
Everybody must get stoned.

5. Well, they'll stone you when you walk all alone.
They'll stone you when you are walking home.
They'll stone you and then say you are brave.
They'll stone you when you are set down in your grave.
But I would not feel so all alone,
Everybody must get stoned.

Pledging My Time

Words and Music by Bob Dylan

10

Visions Of Johanna

Words and Music by Bob Dylan

count-ess who's pre-tend-ing to care for him_ Say-in',

"Name me some-one that's not a par-a-site and I'll_ go out_ and say_ a prayer_

_ for him" But like Lou-ise_ al-ways says_ "Ya can't

look at much,_ can ya man?"As she, her-self, pre-pares for him_

_____ While my con - science ex - plodes The har -
mon - i - cas play _____ the skel - e - ton keys _____ and the rain _____
And these vi - sions _____ of Jo - han - na _____
_____ are now all that _____ re - main. _____

One Of Us Must Know
(Sooner Or Later)

Words and Music by Bob Dylan

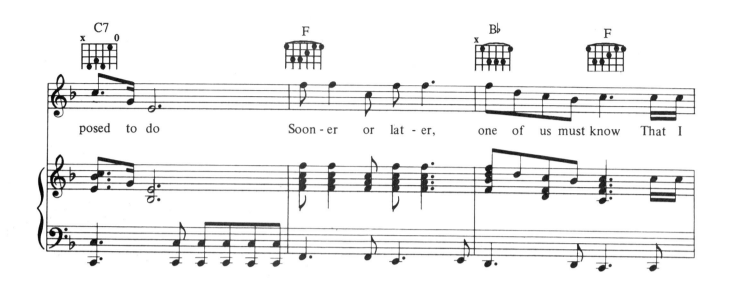

posed to do Soon-er or lat-er, one of us must know That I

real-ly did_try to get close to you

2. I
3. I

I Want You

Words and Music by Bob Dylan

all my fa - thers, they've gone down,_ True love they've_ been with-

out it. But all their daugh - ters put me down 'Cause I don't think a - bout_

_ it.

D.S. al Fine
(3rd and 4th Verses)

3. Well, I re -

Additional Lyrics

3. Well, I return to the Queen of Spades
   And talk with my chambermaid.
   She knows that I'm not afraid
   To look at her.
   She is good to me,
   And there's nothing she doesn't see.
   She knows where I'd like to be,
   But it doesn't matter.
   Chorus

4. Now your dancing child with his Chinese suit,
   He spoke to me, I took his flute.
   No, I wasn't very cute to him,
   Was I?
   But I did it, though, because he lied,
   Because he took you for a ride,
   And because time was on his side,
   And because I ...
   Chorus

Just Like A Woman

Words and Music by Bob Dylan

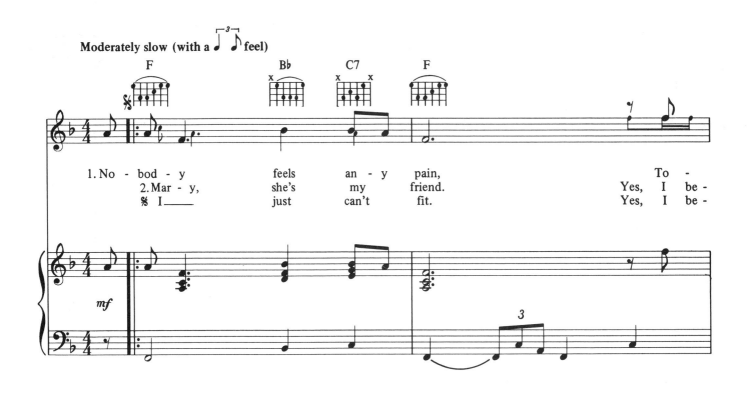

1. No - bod - y feels an - y pain, To -
2. Mar - y, she's my friend. Yes, I be -
   I just can't fit. Yes, I be -

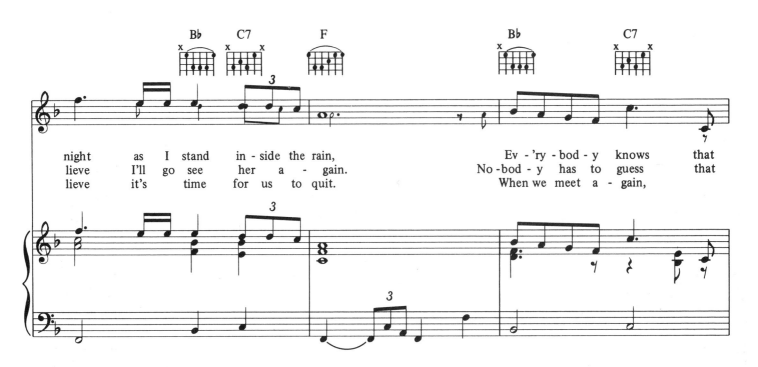

night as I stand in - side the rain, Ev - 'ry - bod - y knows that
lieve I'll go see her a - gain. No - bod - y has to guess that
lieve it's time for us to quit. When we meet a - gain,

Stuck Inside Of Mobile
With The Memphis Blues Again

Words and Music by Bob Dylan

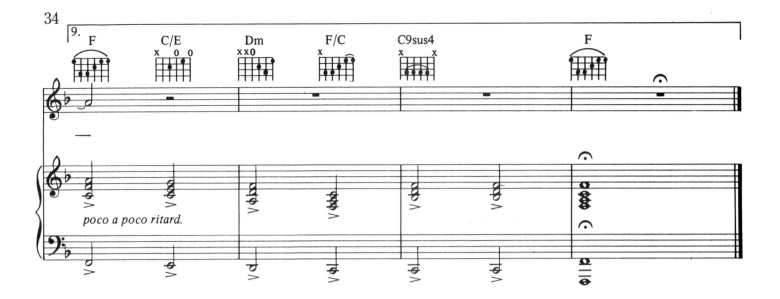

poco a poco ritard.

Additional Lyrics

2. Well, Shakespeare, he's in the alley
   With his pointed shoes and his bells,
   Speaking to some French girl
   Who says she knows me well.
   And I would send a message
   To find out if she's talked,
   But the post office has been stolen
   And the mailbox is locked.
   Chorus

3. Mona tried to tell me
   To stay away from the train line.
   She said that all the railroad men
   Just drink up your blood like wine.
   An' I said, "Oh, I didn't know that,
   But then again, there's only one I've met,
   An' he just smoked my eyelids
   An' punched my cigarette."
   Chorus

4. Grandpa died last week
   And now he's buried in the rocks,
   But everybody still talks about
   How badly they were shocked.
   But me, I expected it to happen,
   I knew he'd lost control
   When he built a fire on Main Street
   And shot it full of holes.
   Chorus

5. Now the senator came down here
   Showing ev'ryone his gun,
   Handing out free tickets
   To the wedding of his son.
   An' me, I nearly got busted,
   An' wouldn't it be my luck
   To get caught without a ticket
   And be discovered beneath a truck.
   Chorus

6. Now the preacher looked so baffled
   When I asked him why he dressed
   With twenty pounds of headlines
   Stapled to his chest.
   But he cursed me when I proved it to him,
   Then I whispered, "Not even you can hide.
   You see, you're just like me,
   I hope you're satisfied."
   Chorus

7. Now the rainman gave me two cures,
   Then he said, "Jump right in."
   The one was Texas medicine,
   The other was just railroad gin.
   An' like a fool I mixed them,
   An' it strangled up my mind.
   An' now people just get uglier,
   An' I have no sense of time.
   Chorus

8. When Ruthie says come see her
   In her honky-tonk lagoon,
   Where I can watch her waltz for free
   'Neath her Panamanian moon,
   An' I say, "Aw come on now,
   You must know about my debutante."
   An' she says, "Your debutante just knows what you need,
   But I know what you want."
   Chorus

9. Now the bricks lay on Grand Street
   Where the neon madmen climb.
   They all fall there so perfectly,
   It all seems so well timed.
   An' here I sit so patiently,
   Waiting to find out what price,
   You have to pay to get out of
   Going through all these things twice.
   Chorus

Leopard-Skin Pill-Box Hat

Words and Music by Bob Dylan

1. Well, I

see you got your___ brand new leop-ard-skin pill - box___ hat___

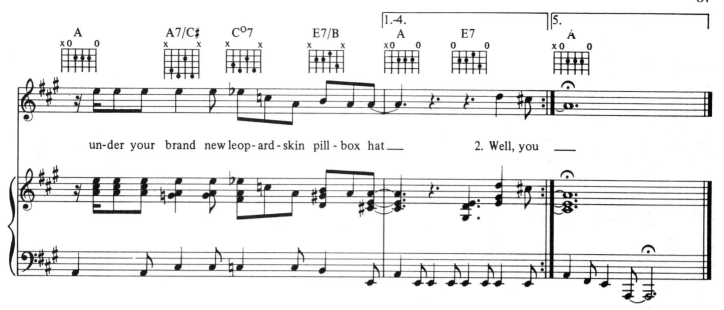

un-der your brand new leop-ard-skin pill-box hat ___   2. Well, you ___

Additional Lyrics

2. Well, you look so pretty in it
   Honey, can I jump on it sometime?
   Yes, I just wanna see
   If it's really that expensive kind
   You know it balances on your head
   Just like a mattress balances
   On a bottle of wine
   Your brand new leopard-skin pill-box hat

3. Well, if you wanna see the sun rise
   Honey, I know where
   We'll go out and see it sometime
   We'll both just sit there and stare
   Me with my belt
   Wrapped around my head
   And you just sittin' there
   In your brand new leopard-skin pill-box hat

4. Well, I asked the doctor if I could see you
   It's bad for your health, he said
   Yes, I disobeyed his orders
   I came to see you
   But I found him there instead
   You know, I don't mind him cheatin' on me
   But I sure wish he'd take that off his head
   Your brand new leopard-skin pill-box hat

5. Well, I see you got a new boyfriend
   You know, I never seen him before
   Well, I saw him
   Makin' love to you
   You forgot to close the garage door
   You might think he loves you for your money
   But I know what he really loves you for
   It's your brand new leopard-skin pill-box hat

Most Likely You Go Your Way
(And I'll Go Mine)

Words and Music by Bob Dylan

But he's bad - ly built And he walks on stilts, Watch out he don't

fall on you.

D. S. al Coda 𝄋

Coda

mine.

Repeat and fade

Repeat and fade

Temporary Like Achilles

Words and Music by Bob Dylan

How come___ you___ don't___ send me no_____ re - gards?_____
How come___ you___ send___ some-one out_____ to have me_____ barred?_____
Just what___ do___ you___ think_____ you have to____ guard?___
How come___ you get some - one like him_____ to be your____ guard?___

You
You
You
You

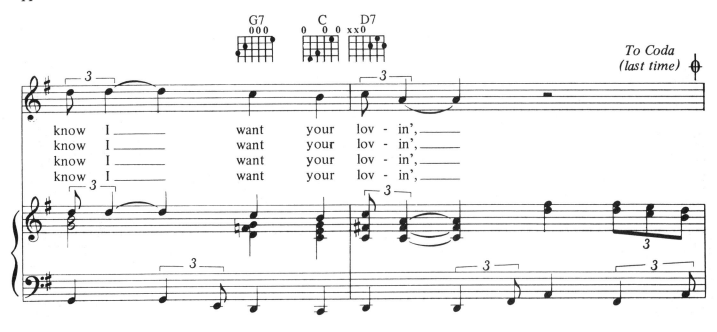

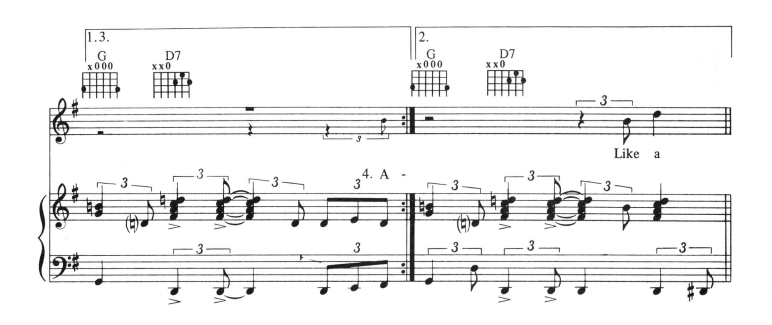

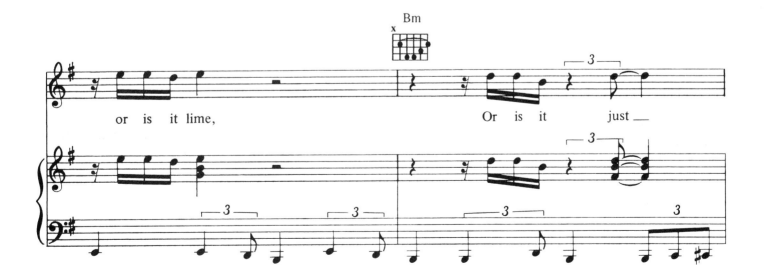

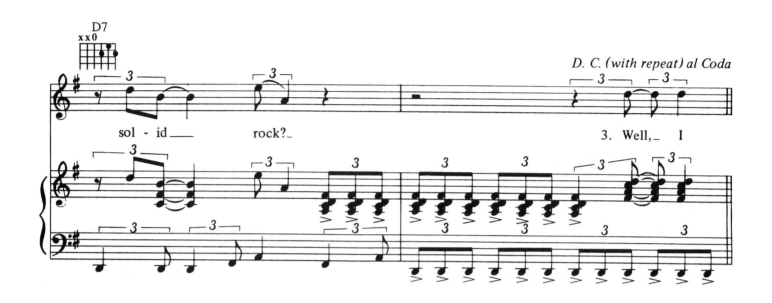

sol - id___ rock?_

3. Well,_ I

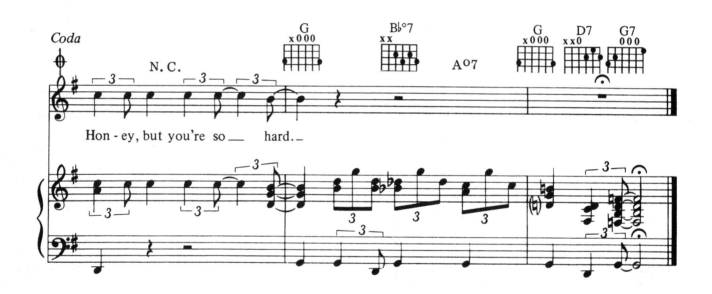

Hon - ey, but you're so___ hard._

Obviously Five Believers

Words and Music by Bob Dylan

I'm call-in' you ___ to
I won't let you ___ down

Please come home ___
No I won't ___

A7

Yes, I guess I could make it with-out you If ___ I
You know I can if you can, hon - ey

E7

D7   No Chord   A7

just did-n't feel ___ so all a - lone.
But, hon-ey, please ___ don't.

2. Don't let me

3. I got my black dog barkin'
   Black dog barkin'
   Yes it is now
   Yes it is now
   Outside my yard
   Yes, I could tell you what he means
   If I just didn't have to try so hard

4. Your mama's workin'
   Your mama's moanin'
   She's cryin' you know
   She's cryin' you know
   You better go now
   Well, I'd tell you what she wants
   But I just don't know how

5. Fifteen jugglers
   Fifteen jugglers
   Five believers
   Five believers
   All dressed like men
   Tell yo' mama not to worry because
   They're just my friends

6. Early in the mornin'
   Early in the mornin'
   I'm callin' you to
   I'm callin' you to
   Please come home
   Yes, I could make it without you
   If I just did not feel so all alone

Fourth Time Around

Words and Music by Bob Dylan

And she worked on __ my
And she buttoned__ her
And after find- ing
She said, _____ "No,
And you, you took __ me

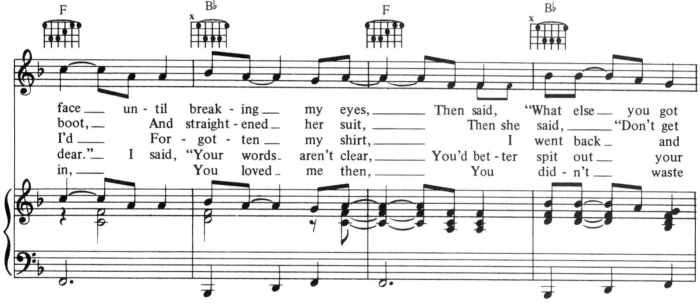

face ___ un - til break- ing __ my eyes, _____ Then said, "What else __ you got
boot, __ And straight- ened __ her suit, _____ Then she said, _____ "Don't get
I'd __ For- got- ten __ my shirt, _____ I went back __ and
dear." I said, "Your words__ aren't clear, _____ You'd bet- ter spit out __ your
in, __ You loved __ me then, _____ You did- n't __ waste

left?"
cute."
knocked.
gum."
time.

It _____ was
So _____ I
I _____
She _____

Absolutely Sweet Marie

Words and Music by Bob Dylan

Moderately, with a beat

Sad-Eyed Lady Of The Lowlands

Words and Music by Bob Dylan

wait? ___

2. With your

Additional Lyrics

2. With your sheets like metal and your belt like lace,
   And your deck of cards missing the jack and the ace,
   And your basement clothes and your hollow face,
   Who among them can think he could **outguess you?**
   With your silhouette when the sunlight dims
   Into your eyes where the moonlight swims,
   And your match-book songs and your gypsy hymns,
   Who among them would try to impress you?
   Chorus

3. The kings of Tyrus with their convict list
   Are waiting in line for their geranium kiss,
   And you wouldn't know it would happen like this,
   But who among them really wants just to kiss you?
   With your childhood flames on your midnight rug,
   And your Spanish manners and your mother's drugs,
   And your cowboy mouth and your curfew plugs,
   Who among them do you think could resist you?
   Chorus

4. Oh, the farmers and the businessmen, they all did decide
   To show you the dead angels that they used to hide.
   But why did they pick you to sympathize with their side?
   Oh, how could they ever mistake you?
   They wished you'd accepted the blame for the farm,
   But with the sea at your feet and the phony false alarm,
   And with the child of a hoodlum wrapped up in your arms,
   How could they ever, ever persuade you?
   Chorus

5. With your sheet-metal memory of Cannery Row,
   And your magazine-husband who one day just had to go,
   And your gentleness now which you just can't help but show,
   Who among them do you think would employ you?
   Now you stand with your thief, you're on his parole
   With your holy medallion which your fingertips fold,
   And your saintlike face and your ghostlike soul,
   Oh, who among them do you think could destroy you?
   Chorus

Nashville Skyline.

Girl From The North Country

Words and Music by Bob Dylan

Additional Lyrics

2. Well if you go in the snowflake storm
   When the rivers freeze and summer ends,
   Please see she has a coat so warm
   To keep her from the howlin' winds.

3. Please see for me if her hair hangs long,
   If it rolls and flows all down her breast,
   Please see for me if her hair hangs long,
   That's the way I remember her best.

4. I'm a-wonderin' if she remembers me at all,
   Many times I've often prayed
   In the darkness of my night,
   In the brightness of my day,

5. So if you're trav'lin' in the north country fair,
   Where the winds hit heavy on the borderline,
   Remember me to one who lives there,
   She once was a true love of mine.

Nashville Skyline Rag

Words and Music by Bob Dylan

Bright Country style

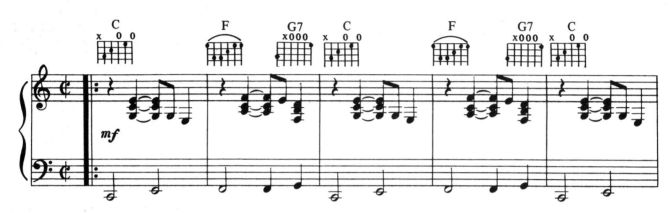

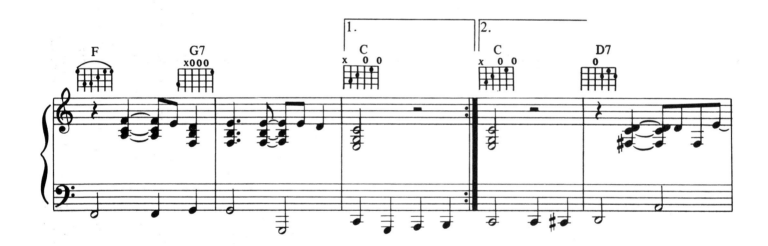

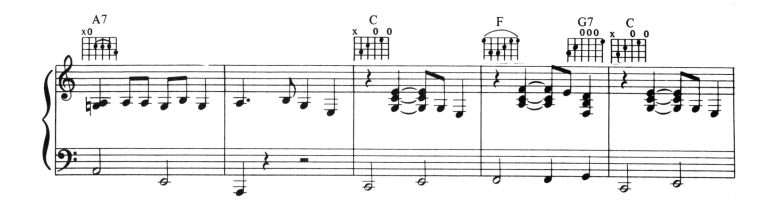

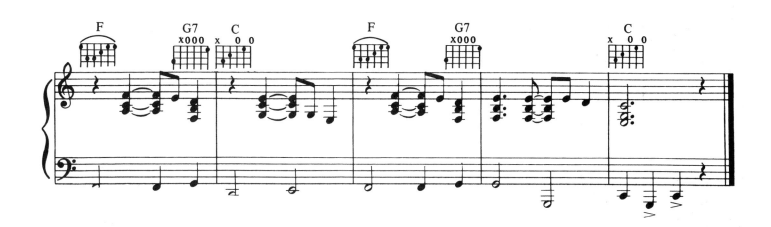

To Be Alone With You

Words and Music by Bob Dylan

73

I Threw It All Away

Words and Music by Bob Dylan

I once held her in my arms, She said she would al-ways stay. But I was cruel, I

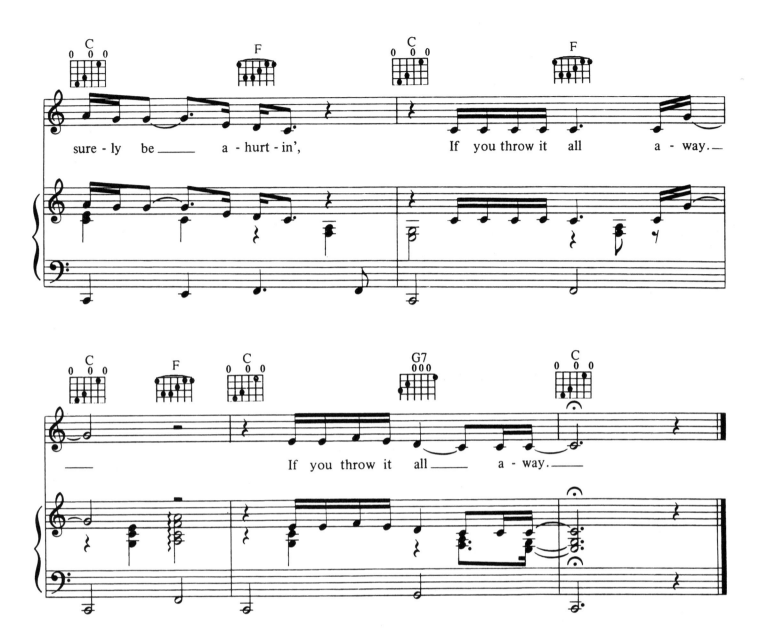

sure - ly be _____ a - hurt - in', If you throw it all a - way. _____

_____ If you throw it all _____ a - way. _____

Peggy Day

Words and Music by Bob Dylan

Peg - gy Day_ stole my poor heart a - way, _
Peg - gy night_ makes my fu - ture look so bright,

By gol - ly, what more can I say, _
Man, that girl_ is out of sight,

Love to spend the night with Peg - gy Day.
Love to spend the day with Peg - gy night.

Well, you know that e - ven be - fore I learned her name, You know I loved her just the same. An'

I tell 'em all, wher - ev - er I may go,___ Just so they'll know, that

she's my lit - tle la - dy And I love ___ her so. ___

Peg - gy Day ___ stole my poor heart a - way, Turned ___

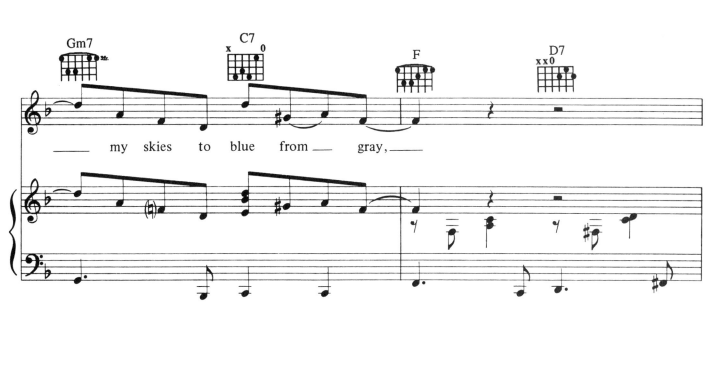

_____ my skies to blue from _____ gray, _____

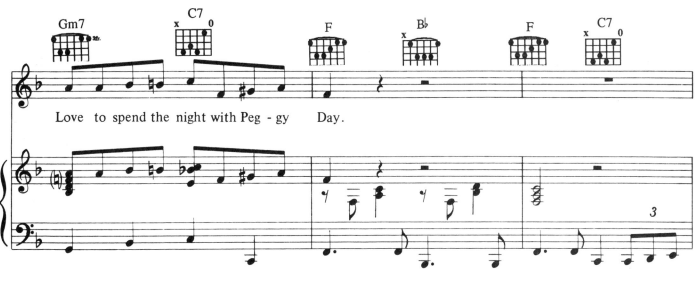

Love to spend the night with Peg - gy Day.

Peg - gy Day _____ stole my poor _____ heart a - way,

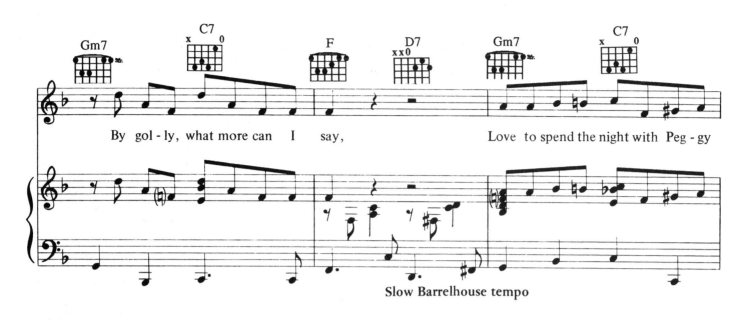

By gol - ly, what more can I say, Love to spend the night with Peg - gy

Slow Barrelhouse tempo

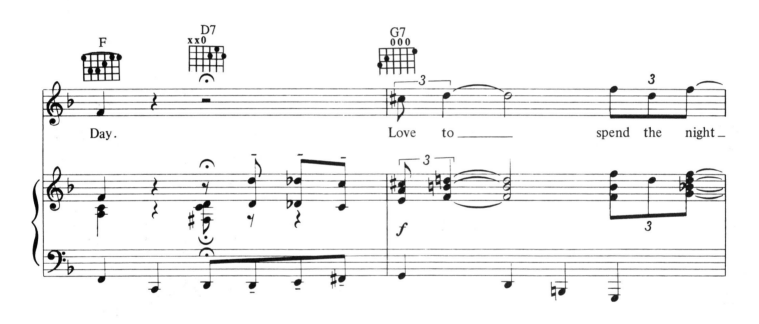

Day. Love to _____ spend the night ___

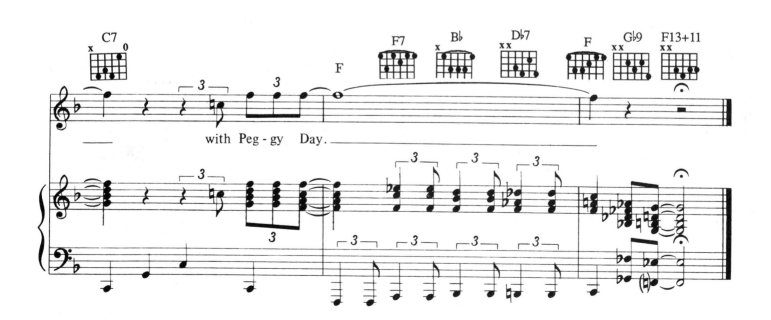

___ with Peg - gy Day. _____

Lay, Lady, Lay

Words and Music by Bob Dylan

You can have your cake___ and eat it too.___

Why wait an - y long - er for___ the one you love,___ When he's stand -

- ing in front of you.___ Lay, la - dy, lay,__

lay a - cross my big brass bed.___ Stay, la - dy, stay,__

One More Night

Words and Music by Bob Dylan

Tell Me That It Isn't True

Words and Music by Bob Dylan

Country Pie

Words and Music by Bob Dylan

Tonight I'll Be Staying Here With You

Words and Music by Bob Dylan

Throw my suit-case out _ there, too,

Throw my trou-bles out the door, I don't

need them an-y more 'Cause to-night I'll be stay-ing here with you.

Blood On The Tracks.

BOB
DYLAN
BLOOD
ON
THE
TRACKS

Tangled Up In Blue

Words and Music by Bob Dylan

Head - ing out for the East__ Coast, Lord

knows I've paid some dues Get - tin' through.__

Tan - gled up in blue.

Additional Lyrics

2. She was married when we first met,
   Soon to be divorced.
   I helped her out of a jam, I guess,
   But I used a little too much force.
   We drove that car as far as we could,
   Abandoned it out West.
   Split up on a dark sad night,
   Both agreeing it was best.
   She turned around to look at me,
   As I was walkin' away.
   I heard her say over my shoulder,
   "We'll meet again some day
   on the avenue."
   Tangled up in blue.

3. I had a job in the great north woods,
   Working as a cook for a spell.
   But I never did like it all that much,
   And one day the axe just fell.
   So I drifted down to New Orleans,
   Where I happened to be employed.
   Workin' for a while on a fishin' boat,
   Right outside of Delacroix.
   But all the while I was alone,
   The past was close behind.
   I seen a lot of women,
   But she never escaped my mind,
   And I just grew.
   Tangled up in blue.

4. She was workin' in a topless place,
   And I stopped in for a beer.
   I just kept lookin' at the side of her face,
   In the spotlight so clear.
   And later on as the crowd thinned out,
   I's just about to do the same.
   She was standing there in back of my chair,
   Said to me, "Don't I know your name?"
   I muttered somethin' underneath my breath,
   She studied the lines on my face.
   I must admit I felt a little uneasy,
   When she bent down to tie the laces
   Of my shoe.
   Tangled up in blue.

5. She lit a burner on the stove,
   And offered me a pipe.
   "I thought you'd never say hello," she said,
   "You look like the silent type."
   Then she opened up a book of poems,
   And handed it to me.
   Written by an Italian poet
   From the thirteenth century.
   And every one of them words rang true,
   And glowed like burnin' coal.
   Pourin' off of every page,
   Like it was written in my soul
   From me to you.
   Tangled up in blue.

6. I lived with them on Montague Street,
   In a basement down the stairs.
   There was music in the cafes at night,
   And revolution in the air.
   Then he started into dealing with slaves,
   And something inside of him died.
   She had to sell everything she owned,
   And froze up inside.
   And when finally the bottom fell out,
   I became withdrawn.
   The only thing I knew how to do,
   Was to keep on keepin' on,
   Like a bird that flew.
   Tangled up in blue.

7. So now I'm goin' back again,
   I got to get to her somehow.
   All the people we used to know,
   They're an illusion to me now.
   Some are mathematicians,
   Some are carpenters' wives.
   Don't know how it all got started,
   I don't know what they're doin' with their lives.
   But me, I'm still on the road,
   Headin' for another joint.
   We always did feel the same,
   We just saw it from a different point
   Of view.
   Tangled up in blue.

If You See Her, Say Hello

Words and Music by Bob Dylan

2. We had a fallin' out
   Like lovers often will
   And to think of how she left that night
   It still brings me a chill
   And though our separation
   It pierced me to the heart
   She still lives inside of me
   We've never been apart

3. If you get close to her
   Kiss her once for me
   I always have respected her
   For busting out and gettin' free
   Oh whatever makes her happy
   I won't stand in the way
   Though the bitter taste still lingers on
   From the night I tried to make her stay

.4. I see a lot of people
   As I make the rounds
   And I hear her name here and there
   As I go from town to town
   And I've never gotten used to it
   I've just learned to turn it off
   Either I'm too sensitive
   Or else I'm gettin' soft

5. Sundown, yellow moon
   I replay the past
   I know every scene by heart
   They all went by so fast
   If she's passin' back this way
   I'm not that hard to find
   Tell her she can look me up
   If she's got the time

You're Gonna Make Me Lonesome When You Go

Words and Music by Bob Dylan

Lily, Rosemary and the Jack of Hearts

Words and Music by Bob Dylan

2. He moved across the mirrored room
"Set it up for everyone," he said
Then everyone commenced to do
What they were doin' before he turned their heads
Then he walked up to a stranger
And he asked him with a grin
"Could you kindly tell me, friend
What time the show begins?"
Then he moved into the corner
Face down like the Jack of Hearts

3. Backstage the girls were playin'
Five card stud by the stairs
Lily had two queens
She was hopin' for a third to match her pair
Outside, the streets were fillin' up
The window was open wide
A gentle breeze was blowin'
You could feel it from inside
Lily called another bet
And drew up the Jack of Hearts

4. Big Jim was no one's fool
He owned the town's only diamond mine
He made his usual entrance
Lookin' so dandy and so fine
With his bodyguards and silver cane
And every hair in place
He took whatever he wanted to
And he laid it all to waste
But his bodyguards and silver cane
Were no match for the Jack of Hearts

5. Rosemary combed her hair
And took a carriage into town
She slipped in through the side door
Lookin' like a queen without a crown
She fluttered her false eyelashes
And whispered in his ear
"Sorry, darlin', that I'm late"
But he didn't seem to hear
He was starin' into space
Over at the Jack of Hearts

6. "I know you've seen that face somewhere,"
Big Jim was thinkin' to himself
"Maybe down in Mexico
Or a picture up on somebody's shelf"
But then the crowd began to stamp their feet
And the house lights did dim
And in the darkness of the room
There was only Jim and him
Starin' at the butterfly
Who just drew the Jack of Hearts

7. Lily was a princess
She was fair-skinned and precious as a child
She did whatever she had to do
She had that certain flash everytime she smiled
She'd come away from a broken home
Had lots of strange affairs
With men in every walk of life
Which took her everywhere
But she'd never met anyone
Quite like the Jack of Hearts

8. The hangin' judge came in
Unnoticed and was being wined and dined
The drillin' in the wall kept up
But no one seemed to pay it any mind
It was known all around
That Lily had Jim's ring
And nothing would ever come between
Lily and the king
No, nothin' ever would
Except maybe the Jack of Hearts

9. Rosemary started drinkin' hard
And seein' her reflection in the knife
She was tired of the attention
Tired of playin' the role of Big Jim's wife
She had done a lot of bad things
Even once tried suicide
Was lookin' to do just one good deed
Before she died
She was gazin' to the future
Riding on the Jack of Hearts

10. Lily washed her face, took her dress off and
Buried it away
"Has your luck run out," she laughed at him
"Well, I guess you must have known it would someday
Be careful not to touch the wall
There's a brand-new coat of paint
I'm glad to see you're still alive
You're lookin' like a saint"
Down the hallway footsteps
Were comin' for the Jack of Hearts

11. The backstage manager
Was pacing all around by his chair
"There's something funny going on,"
He said, "I can just feel it in the air"
He went to get the hangin' judge
But the hangin' judge was drunk
As the leading actor hurried by
In the costume of a monk
There was no actor anywhere
Better than the Jack of Hearts

12. Lily's arms were locked around
    The man that she dearly loved to touch
    She forgot all about
    The man she couldn't stand who hounded her so much
    "I've missed you so," she said to him
    And he felt she was sincere
    But just beyond the door
    He felt jealousy and fear
    Just another night
    In the life of the Jack of Hearts

13. No one knew the circumstance
    But they say that it happened pretty quick
    The door to the dressing room
    Burst open and a cold revolver clicked
    And Big Jim was standin' there
    Ya couldn't say surprised
    Rosemary right beside him
    Steady in her eyes
    She was with Big Jim
    But she was leanin' to the Jack of Hearts

14. Two doors down the boys finally made it
    Through the wall
    And cleaned out the bank safe
    It's said that they got off with quite a haul
    In the darkness by the river bed
    They waited on the ground
    For one more member
    Who had business back in town
    But they couldn't go any further
    Without the Jack of Hearts

15. The next day was hangin' day
    The sky was overcast and black
    Big Jim lay covered up
    Killed by a penknife in the back
    And Rosemary on the gallows
    She didn't even blink
    The hangin' judge was sober
    He hadn't had a drink
    The only person on the scene
    Missin' was the Jack of Hearts

16. The cabaret was empty now
    A sign said, "Closed for repair"
    Lily had already taken
    All of the dye out of her hair
    She was thinkin' 'bout her father
    Who she very rarely saw
    Thinkin' 'bout Rosemary
    And thinkin' about the law
    But most of all
    She was thinkin' 'bout the Jack of Hearts

Shelter From The Storm

Words and Music by Bob Dylan

Idiot Wind

Words and Music by Bob Dylan

blow - ing ev - ery time___ you move___ your teeth._____ You're an

id - i - ot, babe,___ It's a won - der that you still know how to breathe.___

Additional Lyrics

2. I ran into the fortune teller, who said beware of lightning that might strike.
   I haven't know peace and quiet for so long, I can't remember what it's like.
   There's a lone soldier on the cross, smoke pourin' out of a boxcar door.
   You didn't know it, you didn't think it could be done,
       in the final end he won the war after losin' every battle.

   I woke up on the roadside, daydreamin' 'bout the way things sometimes are.
   Visions of you chestnut mare shoot through my head and are makin' me see stars.
   You hurt the ones that I love best and cover up the truth with lies.
   One day you'll be in the ditch, flies buzzin' around your eyes,
       blood on your saddle.

   Idiot wind, blowing through the flowers on your tomb,
   Blowing through the curtains in your room.
   Idiot wind, blowing every time you move your teeth.
   You're an idiot, babe,
   It's a wonder that you still know how to breathe.

3. It was gravity which pulled us down, and destiny which broke us apart.
   You tamed the lion in my cage, but it just wasn't enough to change my heart.
   Now everything's a little upside down,
       as a matter of fact, what's bad is good.
   You'll find out when you reach the top, you're on the bottom.

   I noticed at the ceremony you corrupt ways had finally made you blind.
   I can't remember your face anymore,
       your mouth has changed, your eyes don't look into mine.
   The priest wore black on the seventh day,
       and sat stone-faced while the building burned.
   I waited for you on the running boards near the cypress trees
       while the springtime turned slowly into autumn.

   Idiot wind, blowing like a circle around my skull,
   From the Grand Coulee Dam to the Capitol.
   Idiot wind, blowing every time you move your teeth.
   You're an idiot, babe,
   It's a wonder that you still know how to breathe.

4. I can't feel you anymore, I can't even touch the books you've read.
   Every time I crawl past your door,
       I been wishin' I was somebody else instead.
   Down the highway, down the tracks, down the road to ecstasy,
   I followed you beneath the stars,
       hounded by your memory and all your ragin' glory.

   I been doublecrossed now for the very last time,
       and now I'm finally free.
   I kissed goodbye the howling beast
       on the borderline which separated you from me.
   You'll never know the hurt I suffered not the pain I rise above.
   And I'll never know the same about you, your holiness
       or your kind of love,
   And it makes me feel so sorry.

   Idiot wind, blowing through the buttons of our coats,
   Blowing through the letters that we wrote.
   Idiot wind, blowing through the dust upon our shelves.
   We're idiots, babe,
   It's a wonder we can even feed ourselves.

Meet Me In The Morning

Words and Music by Bob Dylan

Hon - ey we ____ could be in Kan - sas

By time the snow be - gins to thaw. ____

1.- 5.   6.

2. They say the darkest hour
    Is right before the dawn
    They say the darkest hour
    Is right before the dawn
    But you wouldn't know it by me
    Every day's been darkness since you been gone

3. Little rooster crowin'
    There must be something on his mind
    Little rooster crowin'
    There must be something on his mind
    Well I feel just like that rooster
    Honey ya treat me so unkind

4. The birds are flying low, babe
    Honey I feel so exposed
    Well the birds are flying low, babe
    Honey I feel so exposed
    Well now I ain't got any matches
    And the station doors are closed

5. Well I struggled through barbed wire
    Felt the hail fall from above
    Well I struggled through barbed wire
    Felt the hail fall from above
    Well you know I even outran the hound dogs
    Honey you know I've earned your love

6. Look at the sun
    Sinkin' like a ship
    Look at the sun
    Sinkin' like a ship
    Ain't that just like my heart, babe
    When you kissed my lips

Simple Twist Of Fate

Words and Music by Bob Dylan

'Twas then he felt a - lone____ and wished____,

that he'd gone straight,_____ And watched out_____ for a

sim - ple twist of fate._____

They walked a - long by the old_____ ca - nal,____ a lit - tle con - fused, I re -

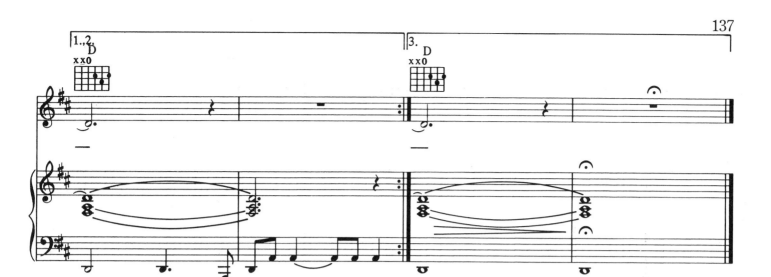

Additional Lyrics

2. A saxophone some place far off played,
   as she was walkin' by the arcade.
   As the light bust through a beat-up shade
   where he was wakin' up,
   She dropped a coin into the cup of a blind man at the gate,
   And forgot about a simple twist of fate.

   He woke up, the room was bare,
   He didn't see her anywhere.
   He told himself he didn't care.
   Pushed the window open wide,
   Felt an emptiness inside to which he just could not relate,
   Brought on by a simple twist of fate.

3. He hears the ticking of the clocks,
   and walks along with a parrot that talks.
   Hunts her down by the waterfront docks
   where the sailors all come in.
   Maybe she'll pick him out again. How long must he wait,
   Once more for a simple twist of fate.

   People tell me it's a sin
   to know and feel too much within.
   I still believe she was my twin,
   but I lost the ring.
   She was born in spring, but I was born too late.
   Blame it on a simple twist of fate.

Buckets Of Rain

Words and Music by Bob Dylan

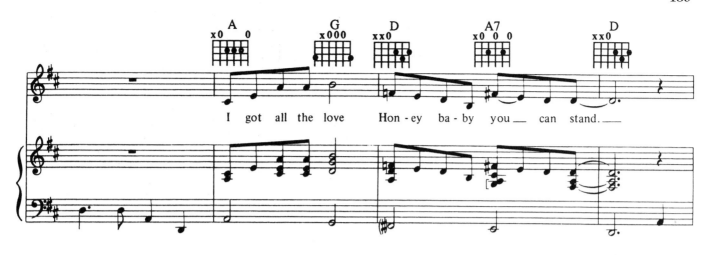

I got all the love Hon-ey ba-by you can stand.

2. I been meek and hard like an oak
   I seen pretty people disappear like smoke
   Friends will arrive
   Friends will disappear
   If you want me
   Honey baby, I'll be here

3. Like your smile and your fingertips
   Like the way that you move your lips
   I like the cool way
   You look at me
   Everything about you
   Is bringing me misery

4. Little red wagon, little red bike
   I ain't no monkey but I know what I like
   I like the way you love me strong and slow
   I'm takin' you with me
   Honey baby, when I go

5. Life is sad, life is a bust
   All ya can do is do what you must
   You do what you must do
   And ya do it well
   I'll do it for you
   Honey baby, can't you tell

You're A Big Girl Now

Words and Music by Bob Dylan

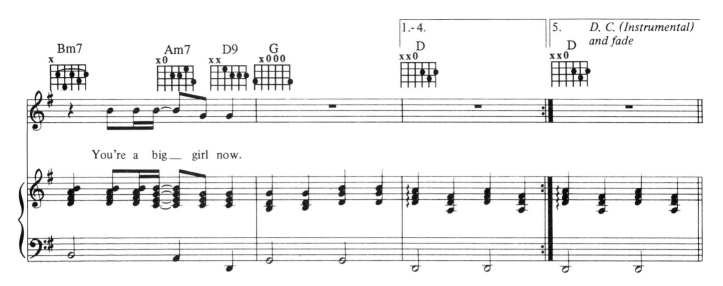

You're a big girl now.

2. Bird on the horizon
Sittin' on a fence
He's singin' his song for me
At his own expense
And I'm just like that bird
Oh-oh
Singin' just for you
I hope that you can hear
Hear me singin' through these tears

3. Time is a jet plane
It moves too fast
Oh, but what a shame
If all we've shared can't last
I can change, I swear
Oh-oh
See what you can do
I can make it through
You can make it too

4. Love is so simple
To quote a phrase
You've known it all the time
I'm learnin' it these days
Oh, I know where I can find you
Oh-oh
In somebody's room
It's a price I have to pay
You're a big girl all the way

5. A change in the weather
Is known to be extreme
But what's the sense of changing
Horses in midstream
I'm going out of my mind
Oh-oh
With a pain that stops and starts
Like a corkscrew to my heart
Ever since we've been apart

Desire.

Hurricane

Music by Bob Dylan
Words by Bob Dylan and Jacques Levy

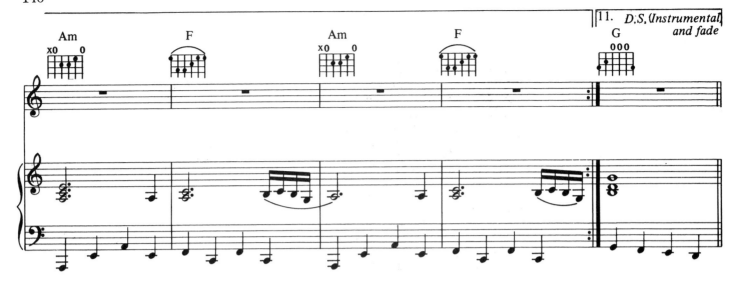

Additional Lyrics

2. Three bodies lyin' there does Patty see,
   And another man named Bello, movin' around mysteriously.
   "I didn't do it," he says, and he throws up his hands,
   "I was only robbin' the register, I hope you understand,
   I saw them leavin'," he says, and he stops.
   "One of us had better call up the cops."
   And so Patty calls the cops,
   And they arrive on the scene with their red lights flashin'
   In the hot New Jersey night.

3. Meanwhile, far away in another part of town,
   Rubin Carter and a couple of friends are drivin' around.
   Number one contender for the middleweight crown,
   Had no idea what kinda shit was about to go down,
   When a cop pulled him over to the side of the road,
   Just like the time before and the time before that.
   In Paterson that's just the way things go,
   If you're black you might as well not show up on the street,
   'Less you wanna draw the heat.

4. Alfred Bello had a partner and he had a rap for the cops,
   Him and Arthur Dexter Bradley were just out prowlin' around.
   He said, "I saw two men runnin' out, they looked like middleweights.
   They jumped into a white car with out-of-state plates."
   And Miss Patty Valentine just nodded her head,
   Cop said, "Wait a minute boys, this one's not dead."
   So they took him to the infirmary,
   And though this man could hardly see,
   They told him that he could identify the guilty men.

5. Four in the mornin' and they haul Rubin in,
   Take him to the hospital and they bring him upstairs.
   The wounded man looks up through his one dyin' eye,
   Says, "Wha'd you bring him in here for? He ain't the guy!"
   Yes, here's the story of the Hurricane,
   The man the authorities came to blame,
   For somethin' that he never done.
   Put in a prison cell, but one time he coulda been
   The champion of the world.

6. **Four months later, the ghettos are in flame,**
   Rubin's in South America, fightin' for his name,
   While Arthur Dexter Bradley's still in the robbery game,
   And the cops are puttin' the screws to him, lookin' for somebody to blame,
   "Remember that murder that happened in a bar?"
   "Remember you said you saw the getaway car?"
   "You think you'd like to play ball with the law?"
   "Think it mighta been that fighter that you saw runnin' that night?"
   "Don't forget that you are white."

7. Arthur Dexter Bradley said, "I'm really not sure,"
   Cops said, "A poor boy like you could use a break.
   We got you for the motel job and we're talkin' to your friend Bello,
   Now you don't wanna have to go back to jail, be a nice fellow.
   You'll be doin' society a favor,
   That sonofabitch is brave and gettin' braver.
   We want to put his ass in stir,
   We want to pin this triple murder on him,
   He ain't no Gentleman Jim."

8. Rubin could take a man out with just one punch,
   But he never did like to talk about it all that much.
   "It's my work," he'd say, "and I do it for pay.
   And when it's over I'd just as soon go on my way,
   Up to some paradise,
   Where the trout streams flow and the air is nice,
   And ride a horse along a trail."
   But then they took him to the jail house,
   Where they try to turn a man into a mouse.

9. All of Rubin's cards were marked in advance,
   The trial was a pig-circus, he never had a chance.
   The judge made Rubin's witnesses drunkards from the slums,
   To the white folks who watched he was a revolutionary bum.
   And to the black folks he was just a crazy nigger,
   No one doubted that he pulled the trigger,
   And though they could not produce the gun,
   The D. A. said he was the one who did the deed.
   And the all-white jury agreed.

10. Rubin Carter was falsely tried,
    The crime was murder-one, guess who testified?
    Bello and Bradley, and they both baldly lied,
    And the newspapers, they all went along for the ride.
    How can the life of such a man
    Be in the palm of some fool's hand?
    To see him obviously framed,
    Couldn't help but make me feel ashamed to live in a land
    Where justice is a game.

11. Now all the criminals in their coats and their ties
    Are free to drink martinis and watch the sun rise,
    While Rubin sits like Buddha in a ten-foot cell,
    An innocent man in a living hell.
    That's the story of the Hurricane,
    But it won't be over till they clear his name,
    And give him back the time he's done,
    Put in a prison cell, but one time he coulda been
    The champion of the world.

Black Diamond Bay

Music by Bob Dylan
Words by Bob Dylan and Jacques Levy

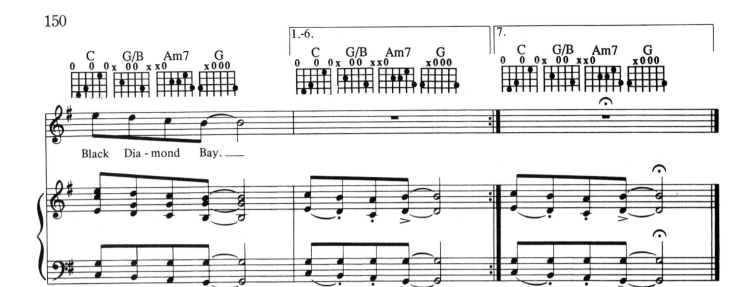

Black Dia-mond Bay.

2. As the mornin' light breaks open
The Greek comes down and he asks for a rope and a
Pen that will write
"Pardon, Monsieur," the desk clerk says
Carefully removes his fez
"Am I hearin' you right?"
And as the yellow fog is liftin'
The Greek is quickly
Headin' for the second floor
She passes him on the spiral staircase
Thinkin' he's the
Soviet Ambassador
She starts to speak
But he walks away
As the storm clouds rise and the palm branches sway
On Black Diamond Bay

3. A soldier sits beneath the fan
Doin' business with a tiny man who
Sells him a ring
Lightning strikes, the lights blow out
The desk clerk wakes and begins to shout
"Can you see anything?"
Then the Greek appears on the second floor
In his bare feet with a
Rope around his neck
While a loser in the gambling room
Lights up a candle, says
"Open up another deck"
But the dealer says
"Attendez-vous, s'il vous plaît"
As the rain beats down and the cranes fly away
From Black Diamond Bay

4. The desk clerk heard the woman laugh
As he looked around in the aftermath
And the soldier got tough
He tried to grab the woman's hand
Said, "Here's a ring, it cost a grand." She said
"That ain't enough"
Then she ran upstairs to pack her bags
While a horse-drawn taxi
Waited at the curb
She passed the door that the Greek had locked
Where a hand-written sign read
"Do Not Disturb"
She knocked upon it anyway
As the sun went down and the music did play
On Black Diamond Bay

5. "I've got to talk to someone quick!"
But the Greek said, "Go away," and he kicked the
Chair to the floor
He hung there from the chandelier
She cried, "Help, there's danger near, please
Open up the door!"
Then the volcano erupted
And the lava flowed down
From the mountain high above
The soldier and the tiny man
Were crouched in the corner
Thinking of forbidden love
But the desk clerk said
"It happens every day"
As the stars fell down and the fields burned away
On Black Diamond Bay

6. As the island slowly sank
The loser finally broke the bank
In the gambling room
The dealer said
"It's too late now
You can take your money
But I don't know how you'll
Spend it in the tomb"
The tiny man bit the soldier's ear
As the floor caved in and
The boiler in the basement blew
While she's out on the balcony
Where a stranger tells her
"My darling, je vous aime beaucoup"
She sheds a tear and then begins to pray
As the fire burns on and the smoke drifts away
From Black Diamond Bay

7. I was sittin' home alone one night
In L.A. watchin' old Cronkite on the
Seven o'clock news
It seems there was an earthquake that
Left nothin' but a Panama hat
And a pair of old Greek shoes
Didn't seem like much was happenin'
So I turned it off and
Went to grab another beer
Seems like every time you turn around
There's another hard luck
Story that you're gonna hear
And there's really nothin'
Anyone can say
And I never did plan to go anyway
To Black Diamond Bay

Mozambique

Words and Music by Bob Dylan and Jacques Levy

Oh, Sister

Music by Bob Dylan
Words by Bob Dylan and Jacques Levy

One More Cup Of Coffee
(Valley Below)

Words and Music by Bob Dylan

pil-low where you lie ___ But I don't sense af - fec - tion ___

No grat - i - tude or love ___ Your loy - al - ty is not to me ___ But

to the stars a - bove ___ One more cup of cof - fee for the road ___

___ One more cup of cof - fee 'fore I go ___

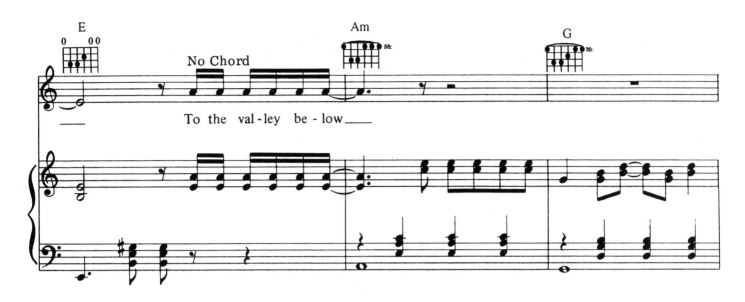

To the val - ley be - low____

2. Your
3. Your

2. Your daddy he's an outlaw
And a wanderer by trade
He'll teach you how to pick and choose
And how to throw the blade
He oversees his kingdom
So no stranger does intrude
His voice it trembles as he calls out for
Another plate of food

One more cup of coffee for the road
One more cup of coffee 'fore I go
To the valley below

3. Your sister sees the future
Like your mama and yourself
You've never learned to read or write
There's no books upon your shelf
And your pleasure knows no limits
Your voice is like a meadow lark
But your heart is like an ocean
Mysterious and dark

One more cup of coffee for the road
One more cup of coffee 'fore I go
To the valley below

Isis

Music by Bob Dylan
Words by Bob Dylan and Jacques Levy

1. I married Isis on the fifth day of May, But I could not hold on to her very long. So I cut off my

2. I came to a high place of darkness and light.
The dividing line ran through the center of town.
I hitched up my pony to a post on the right,
Went into the laundry to wash my clothes down.

3. A man in the corner approached me for a match.
I knew right away he was not ordinary.
He said, "Are you lookin' for somethin' easy to catch?"
I said, "I got no money." He said, "That ain't necessary."

4. We set out that night for the cold in the North.
I gave him my blanket, he gave me his word.
I said, "Where are we goin'?" He said we'd be back by the fourth.
I said, "That's the best news that I've ever heard."

5. I was thinkin' about turquoise, I was thinkin' about gold,
I was thinkin' about diamonds and the world's biggest necklace.
As we rode through the canyons, through the devilish cold,
I was thinkin' about Isis, how she thought I was so reckless.

6. How she told me that one day we would meet up again,
   And things would be different the next time we wed,
   If only I could hang on and just be her friend.
   I still can't remember all the best things she said.

7. We came to the pyramids all embedded in ice.
   He said, "There's a body I'm tryin' to find,
   If I carry it out, it'll bring a good price."
   'Twas then that I knew what he had on his mind.

8. The wind it was howlin' and the snow was outrageous.
   We chopped through the night and we chopped through the dawn.
   When he died I was hopin' that it wasn't contagious,
   But I made up my mind that I had to go on.

9. I broke into the tomb, but the casket was empty.
   There was no jewels, no nothin', I felt I'd been had.
   When I saw that my partner was just bein' friendly,
   When I took up his offer I must-a been mad.

10. I picked up his body and I dragged him inside,
    Threw him down in the hole and I put back the cover.
    I said a quick prayer and I felt satisfied.
    Then I rode back to find Isis just to tell her that I love her.

11. She was there in the meadow where the creek used to rise.
    Blinded by sleep and in need of a bed,
    I came in from the East with the sun in my eyes.
    I cursed her one time then I rode on ahead.

12. She said, "Where ya been?" I said, "No place special."
    She said, "You look different," I said, "Well, I guess."
    She said, "You been gone." I said, "That's only natural."
    She said, "You gonna stay?" I said, "If ya want me to, yes."

13. Isis, oh, Isis, you mystical child.
    What drives me to you is what drives me insane.
    I still can remember the way that you smiled
    On the fifth day of May in the drizzlin' rain.

Sara

Words and Music by Bob Dylan

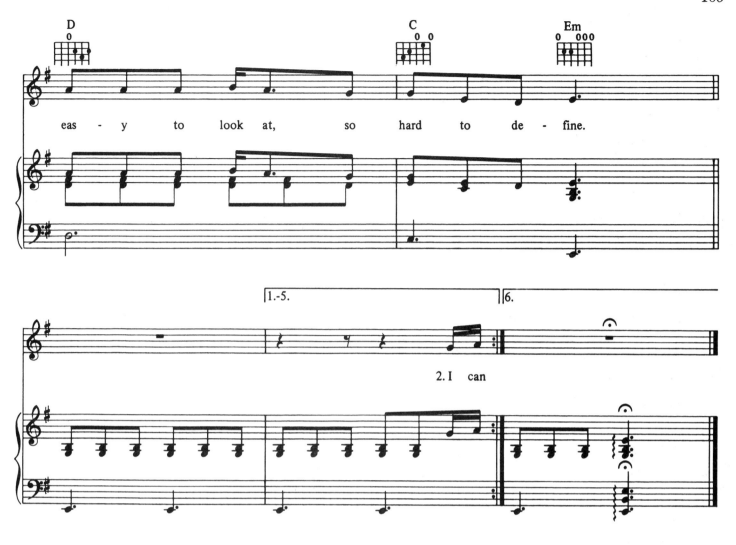

eas - y to look at, so hard to de - fine.

1.-5.

6.

2. I can

Additional Lyrics

2. I can still see them playin'
   With their pails in the sand,
   They run to the water
   Their buckets to fill.
   I can still see the shells
   Fallin out of their hands,
   As they follow each other
   Back up the hill.

   Sara, Sara,
   Sweet virgin angel, sweet love of my life.
   Sara, Sara,
   Radiant jewel, mystical wife.

3. Sleepin' in the woods
   By a fire in the night,
   Drinkin' white rum
   In a Portugal bar.
   Them playin' leap-frog
   And hearin' about Snow White,
   You in the marketplace
   In Savanna-la-Mar.

   Sara, Sara,
   It's all so clear, I could never forget.
   Sara, Sara,
   Lovin' you is the one thing I'll never regret.

4. I can still hear the sounds
   Of those Methodist bells,
   I'd taken the cure
   And had just gotten through.
   Stayin' up for days
   In the Chelsea Hotel,
   Writin' "Sad-Eyed Lady
   Of the Lowlands" for you.

   Sara, Sara,
   Wherever we travel we're never apart.
   Sara, oh Sara,
   Beautiful lady, so dear to my heart.

5. How did I met you,
   I don't know,
   A messenger sent me
   In a tropical storm.
   You were there in the winter,
   Moonlight on the snow,
   And on Lily Pond Lane
   When the weather was warm.

   Sara, oh Sara,
   Scorpio Sphinx in a calico dress.
   Sara, Sara,
   You must forgive me my unworthiness.

6. Now the beach is deserted
   Exept for some kelp,
   And a piece of an old ship
   That lies on the shore.
   You always responded
   When I needed your help,
   You gimme a map
   And a key to your door.

   Sara, oh Sara,
   Glamorous nymph with an arrow and bow.
   Sara, oh Sara,
   Don't ever leave me, don't ever go.

Joey

Music by Bob Dylan
Words by Bob Dylan and Jacques Levy

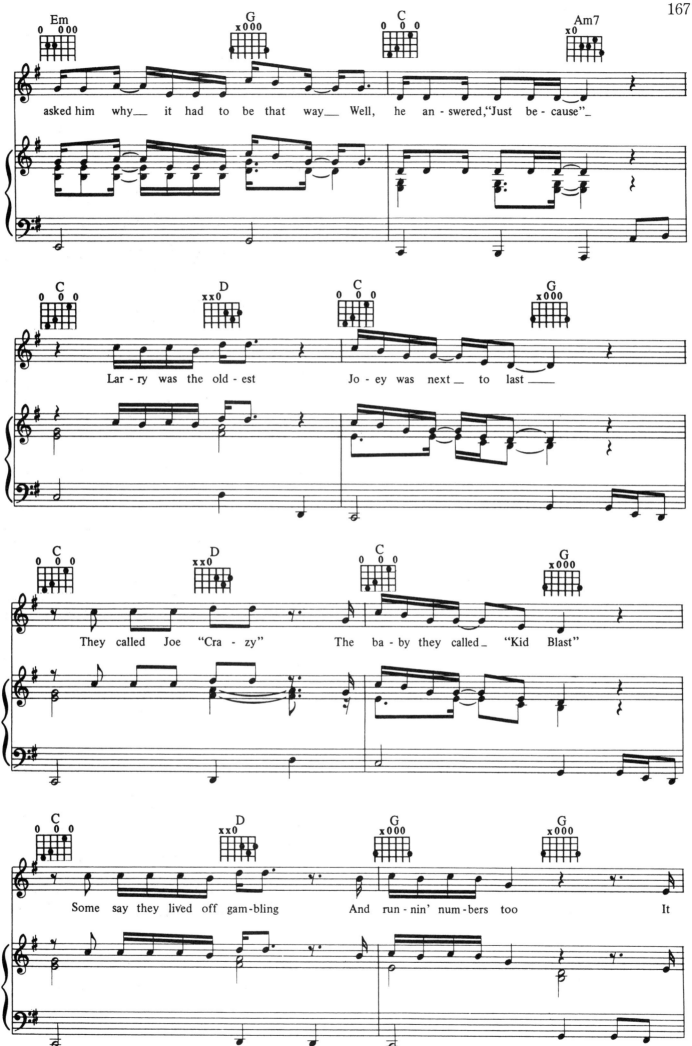

asked him why__ it had to be that way__ Well, he an-swered,"Just be-cause"__

Lar-ry was the old-est   Jo-ey was next__ to last _____

They called Joe "Cra-zy"   The ba-by they called__ "Kid Blast"

Some say they lived off gam-bling   And run-nin' num-bers too   It

al - ways seemed they got caught be - tween The mob and the men in blue

(Vocal harmony) Jo - ey, Jo - ey King of the streets,

child of clay Jo - ey, Jo - ey

What made them want to come and blow you a - way?

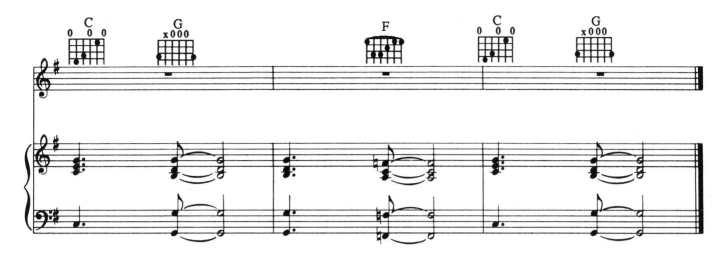

2. There was talk they killed their rivals
   But the truth was far from that
   No one ever knew for sure
   Where they were really at
   When they tried to strangle Larry
   Joey almost hit the roof
   He went out that night to seek revenge
   Thinkin' he was bullet-proof

   The war broke out at the break of dawn
   It emptied out the streets
   Joey and his brothers
   Suffered terrible defeats
   Till they ventured out behind the lines
   And took five prisoners
   They stashed them away in a basement
   Called them amateurs

   The hostages were tremblin'
   When they heard a man exclaim
   "Let's blow this place to Kingdom Come
   Let Con Edison take the blame"
   But Joey stepped up, he raised his hand
   Said, "We're not those kind of men
   It's peace and quiet that we need
   To go back to work again"

   Joey, Joey
   King of the streets, child of clay
   Joey, Joey
   What made them want to come and blow you away?

4. It was true that in his later years
   He would not carry a gun
   "I'm around too many children," he'd say
   "They should never know of one"
   Yet he walked right into the clubhouse
   Of his life-long deadly foe
   Emptied out the register
   Said, "Tell 'em it was Crazy Joe"

   One day they blew him down
   In a clam bar in New York
   He could see it comin' through the door
   As he lifted up his fork
   He pushed the table over
   To protect his family
   Then he staggered out into the streets
   Of Little Italy

   Joey, Joey
   King of the streets, child of clay
   Joey, Joey
   What made them want to come and blow you away?

3. The police department hounded him
   They called him Mr. Smith
   They got him on conspiracy
   They were never sure who with
   "What time is it?" said the judge
   To Joey when they met
   "Five to ten," said Joey
   The judge says, "That's exactly what you get"

   He did ten years in Attica
   Reading Nietzsche and Wilhelm Reich
   They threw him in the hole one time
   For tryin' to stop a strike
   His closest friends were black men
   'Cause they seemed to understand
   What it's like to be in society
   With a shackle on your hand

   When they let him out in '71
   He'd lost a little weight
   But he dressed like Jimmy Cagney
   And I swear he did look great
   He tried to find the way back in
   To the life he left behind
   To the boss he said, "I have returned
   And now I want what's mine."

   Joey, Joey
   King of the streets, child of clay
   Joey, Joey
   Why did they have to come and blow you away?

5. Sister Jacqueline and Carmela
   And Mother Mary all did weep
   I heard his best friend Frankie say
   "He ain't dead, he's just asleep."
   Then I saw the old man's limousine
   Head back towards the grave
   I guess he had to say one last goodbye
   To the son that he could not save

   The sun turned cold over President Street
   And the town of Brooklyn mourned
   They said a mass in the old church
   Near the house where he was born
   And someday if God's in heaven
   Overlookin' his preserve
   I know the men that shot him down
   Will get what they deserve

   Joey, Joey
   King of the streets, child of clay
   Joey, Joey
   What made them want to come and blow you away?

Romance In Durango

Music by Bob Dylan
Words by Bob Dylan and Jacques Levy

1. Hot chil - i pep - pers in the blis - ter - ing sun,____

Dust on my face ____ and my cape.____

Me and Mag - da - le - na on ____ the run,____

2. Past the Aztec ruins and the ghosts of our people.
    Hoofbeats like castanets on stone.
    At night I dream of bells in the village steeple,
    Then I see the bloody face of Ramon.

    Was it me that shot him down in the cantina?
    Was it my hand that held the gun?
    Come, let us fly, my Magdalena,
    The dogs are barking and what's done is done.

    No llores, mi querida,
    Dios nos vigila,
    Soon the horse will take us to Durango.
    Agarrame, mi vida,
    Soon the desert will be gone.
    Soon you will be dancing the fandango.

3. At the corrida we'll sit in the shade
    And watch the young torero stand alone.
    We'll drink tequila where our grandfathers stayed
    When they rode with Villa into Toreon.

    Then the padre will recite the prayers of old
    In the little church this side of town.
    I will wear new boots and an earring of gold.
    You'll shine with diamonds in your wedding gown.

    The way is long but the end is near.
    Already the fiesta has begun.
    The face of God will appear
    With His serpent eyes of obsidian.

    No llores, mi querida,
    Dios nos vigila,
    Soon the horse will take us to Durango.
    Agarrame, mi vida,
    Soon the desert will be gone.
    Soon you will be dancing the fandango.

4. Was that the thunder that I heard?
    My head is vibrating, I feel a sharp pain.
    Come sit by me, don't say a word.
    Oh, can it be that I am slain!

    Quick, Magdalena, take my gun.
    Look, up in the hills, that flash of light!
    Aim well, my little one,
    We may not make it through the night.

    No llores, mi querida,
    Dios nos vigila,
    Soon the horse will take us to Durango.
    Agarrame, mi vida,
    Soon the desert will be gone.
    Soon you will be dancing the fandango.